THE D

by John Montague

POETRY

Forms of Exile (1959)

Poisoned Lands (1961, 1977)

A Chosen Light (1967)

Tides (1970)

The Rough Field (1972)

A Slow Dance (1975)

The Great Cloak (1978)

Selected Poems (1982)

EDITED:

The Faber Book of Irish Verse (1974)

PROSE

Death of a Chieftain (1964, 1977)

JOHN MONTAGUE

THE DEAD KINGDOM

El reino muerto vive todavia.
    Pablo Neruda

THE DOLMEN PRESS

BLACKSTAFF PRESS

OXFORD UNIVERSITY PRESS

Set in Palatino type by Redsetter Limited
and printed in the Republic of Ireland by Irish Printers Limited
for the publishers,
The Dolmen Press Limited, Mountrath, Portlaoise, Ireland
in association with
Wake Forest University Press
Winston-Salem, North Carolina 27109, USA

Blackstaff Press Limited
3 Galway Park, Dundonald, BT16OAN
and
Oxford University Press, Walton Street, Oxford OX2 6DP
London Glasgow New York Toronto
Delhi Bombay Calcutta Madras Karachi Kuala Lumpur
Singapore Hong Kong Tokyo Nairobi Dar es Salaam
Cape Town Melbourne Auckland
and associates in
Beirut Berlin Ibadan Mexico City Nicosia
CANADA: Exile Editions, Toronto.

Designed by Liam Miller

First published 1984

British Library Cataloguing in Publication Data
  Montague, John
  The dead kingdom.
  I. Title
  821'.914   PR6063.05

ISBN 0-85105-395-5 The Dolmen Press
ISBN 0-85640-312-1 Blackstaff Press
ISBN 0-19-211961-3 Oxford University Press

© 1984: John Montague

The Dolmen Press receives financial assistance from
The Arts Council, An Comhairle Ealaíon, Ireland.

Copyright under the Berne Convention, all rights reserved. Apart from fair dealing for study or review, no part of this publication may be reproduced, stored in a retrieval system or transmitted, in any form or by any means, electronic, mechanical, photocopying, recording, or otherwise, without the prior permission of The Dolmen Press.

This book is sold subject to the condition that it shall not, by way of trade or otherwise, be lent, re-sold, hired out or otherwise circulated without the publisher's prior consent in any form of binding or cover other than that in which it is published and without a similar condition including this condition being imposed on the subsequent purchaser.

CONTENTS

I: UPSTREAM

Upstream 11
A Murmuring Stream 13
A Last Gesture 15
Abbeylara 16
Process 18
Gone 19
Invocation to the Guardian 20

II: THIS NEUTRAL REALM

Bog Royal 25
A Slight Fragrance 27
Red Island 29
Lake Dwelling: Crannóg 31
Swordland 33
This Neutral Realm 34
The Music Box 36
The Well Dreams 38

III: THE BLACK PIG

The Black Pig 43
Border Lake 44
Border 45
The Plain of Blood 47
The Web of Man (*A Curse*) 49

Red Branch (*A Blessing*) 50

Wintry Dawn 52

Deities 54

IV: THE SILVER FLASK

Gravity 59

Northern Express 61

Intimacy 62

Molly Bawn 64

A Muddy Cup 66

Christmas Card 69

At Last 71

The Silver Flask 72

Last Journey 74

What a View 76

V: A FLOWERING ABSENCE

Family Conference 83

Procession 84

Northern Lights 86

A Flowering Absence 89

The Locket 92

A New Litany 94

Back 96

The images which precede the sections are reproduced with acknowledgements to their sources. The Sheela-na-gig from Cavan (p.7) is from the National Museum of Ireland; the Egyptian Ship of the Dead (p.9) and the Viking prow (p.23) are from the British Museum; the engraving of Brooklyn Bridge is from a contemporary paper.

THE DEAD KINGDOM

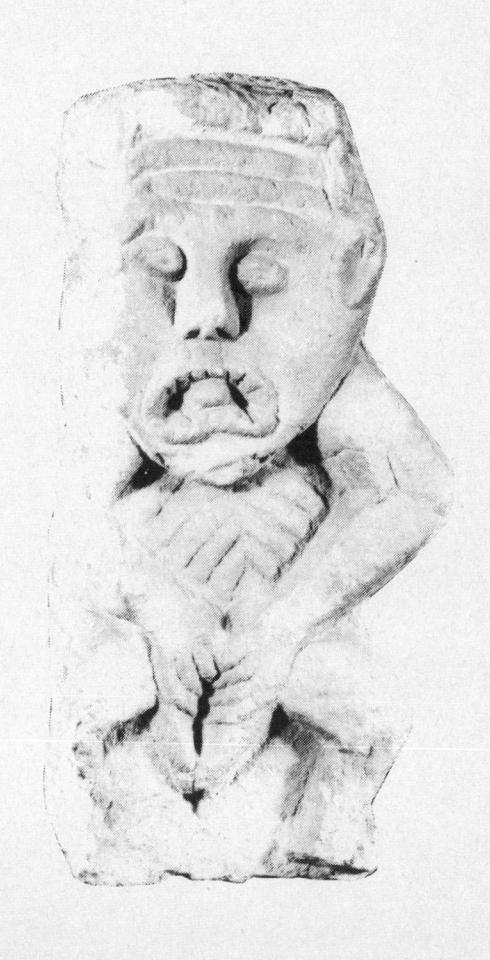

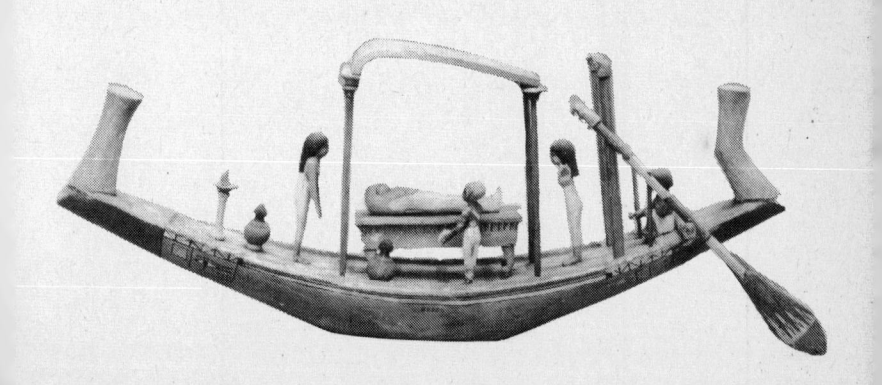

I

UPSTREAM

"There is no permanence. Do we build a house to stand for
ever, do we seal a contract to hold for all time? Do
brothers divide an inheritance to keep for ever, does the
flood-time of rivers endure? It is only the nymph of the
dragon-fly who sheds her larva and sees the sun in his
glory. From the days of old there is no permanence.
The sleeping and the dead, how alike they are, they are like
a painted death. What is there between the master and the
servant when both have fulfilled their doom? When the
judges come together, and the mother ot destinies,
together they decree the fates of men. Life and death
they allot but the day of death they do not disclose."

> *The Book of Gilgamesh:*
> *Written down according to the original and*
> *collated in the palace of*
> *Ashurbanipal, King of the World.*

"And you have no part in the other world?" asked the
Burgomeister, knitting his brows.
"I am forever," replied the hunter, "on the great stair that
leads up to it. On that infinitely wide and spacious stair
I clamber about, sometimes up, sometimes down, sometimes
on the right, sometimes on the left, always in motion.
The hunter has been changed into a butterfly."

> Franz Kafka

UPSTREAM

Northwards, annually,
a journeying back,
the salmon's leap
& pull to the source:
my wife, from the shore
at Roche's Point, calls
*John, come in, come home,
your mother is dead.*

We pull the curragh
into shallow water,
haul her above tide
level, two sets of lean
insect legs stumbling
up the stony beach,
the curve of the boat
heavy on our napes
before we lift her
high on the trestles,
then store the long,
light oars, deliberately
neat and calm in crisis,
keeping the mind busy.

Under the lighthouse dome
the strangeness of Evelyn
weeping for someone
she has never known —
her child's grandmother —
while I stand, dryeyed,
phoning and phoning a cousin
until, cursing, I turn
to feel his shadow loom
across the threshold.

[11]

Secret, lonely messages
along the air, older than
humming telephone wires,
blood talk, neglected
affinities of family,
antennae of instinct
reaching through space,
first intelligence.

(The night O Riada dies
a friend wakes up in
the South of France,
*feeling a great lightness,
a bird taking off.*)

A MURMURING STREAM

Now Brendan sits silently
beside me in his car as
we drive through the long
monotony of our Midlands;
minor roads of memory
leading past a stone keep
stranded by history,
an ivy strangled abbey
near his first home
where unemployed play
pitch and toss above
a murmuring stream
and a handball cracks
against tall concrete
while a ballad rises:
Sweet Nelly Dean!

My own memories as well:
wartime summers in this
sluggish, forgotten world,
chugging turf-fed trains,
Goldsmithian simplicities
of teacher and priest,
a tangled lane winding
to the hidden sweetness
of a whitewashed well
with, beyond the scringing
stile to the chapel,
wide, hedgeless fields
where I raced naked
under bent crab trees,
or pressed my body upon
the loam scented earth.

Triumphantly carrying home
trophies from the stream,
jamjars of fresh water,
flecked with green weed,
in which minnows twisted
and turned in prison, or
stared out, enlarged
to gross-eyed monsters,
mouths kneading....

A LAST GESTURE
I.M. Mary O Meara

When his mother died,
her face calm, despite
great pain, she scorned
any false consolation —
I'm done, she repeated,
thinking only of the man
she had looked after
all their life, lying
in hospital, while she
drifted slowly down,
powerless to comfort,
no longer his woman,
resigning the human.

Before he was taken
away, he went again
to the well, laboriously
fetching her a can
of fresh spring water.
Her first food for days,
she found it tasted
sweet and chill, with
a trail and smell of
green seeping through
the acrid tinge
of metal. And praised
his last gesture,
saying, *he was right:*
its sweetness did me good.

ABBEYLARA

In the garden at Abbeylara
it was always summer,
bees fumbling the lilac,
the pink & white blossoms
of the flowering potatoes,
and here Uncle John comes,
fussily patting the drills
with the flat of his spade
while Aunt Mary reaches
over nestling hens, nettles
to where soft raspberries
loosen on a spiky stem,
or gathers into her apron
tart pellets of currants,
gross, hairy gooseberries
to explode on the tongue.

In the house at Abbeylara
it was always busy & warm,
Uncle John bending down to
pat a terrier with eyebrows
as bushy as his own, or
crackling his newspaper,
*"I saw Mick Collins once,
black haired and laughing,
they shouldn't have shot him."*
Aunt Mary baking a scone
or rounding the crust on
a thick appletart while
the children cranked up
the great horned gramophone,
the tremulous melancholy
of Count McCormack's
silvery tongue soaring in

Kathleen Mavourneen, or
*an old rustic bridge that
bends o'er a murmuring stream.*
Now they are both gone.
Months after their funerals
Brendan drives from Dublin,
to break, like a burglar,
into his old home, collect
stale documents, photographs.
The house smelt of neglect
and the garden was overrun;
crumbling unpicked berries
bending the tangled stems:
a small cleared realm
reverting to first chaos
as if they had never been.

PROCESS

The structure of process,
time's gullet devouring
parents whose children
are swallowed in turn,
families, houses, towns,
built or battered down,
only the earth and sky
unchanging in change,
everything else fragile
as a wild bird's wing;
bulldozer and butterfly,
dogrose and snowflake
climb the unending stair
into God's golden eye.

Each close in his own
world of sense & memory,
races, nations locked
in their dream of history,
only love or friendship,
an absorbing discipline
(the healing harmony
of music, painting, poem)
as swaying ropeladders
across fuming oblivion
while the globe turns,
and the stars turn, and
the great circles shine,
gold & silver,

      sun & moon.

GONE

So sing a song for
things that are gone,
minute and great,
celebrated, unknown.

The library of Alexandria,
the swaying Howth tram,
the royal city of Hue,
the pub of Phil Ryan.

Hovering fifty, I
have seen substantial things
hustled into oblivion:
castles, branchlines,

The Clogher Valley
railway bustling along
the hedges of Tyrone,
a Hornby toy train.

Tall walls of Dublin
dishonoured and torn;
Belfast's Victorian villas,
rose windows of the Crown;

Like the Great Forests
of Ireland, hacked down
to uphold the Jacobean
houses of London:

Chiding Spenser, I yet sing
of the goddess Mutability,
dark Lady of Process,
our devouring Queen.

INVOCATION TO THE GUARDIAN

Master of royal decorum
Great Lord of Babylon,
Excelling in the javelin,
Drawing of the long bow,
Charioteering, lion spearing;

All powers in the realm,
Both physical and mental,
Swift resolver of problems
With no apparent solution;
Who could read the tablets
In abstruse Sumerian. Sir,

Legendary as Nimrod of Nineveh
Swift as Macedon's Alexander,
At twenty, the 'hegemon', benevolent
As the Buddha struck Ashoka,
Scholarly as Cormac of Cashel,
Wise as Justinian, brisk
As that codifying Corsican;

Who gave your craftsmen
Their dazzling freedom,
The hollow bronze lion
Crouched ready to spring,
The human headed scorpion;

I have seen your workroom,
Admired your quiet handling
Of some impossible problem,
Moving from point to point

Unperturbed by admiration,
So selflessly absorbed in
The task to hand, climbing
The ladder to defy oblivion:

Stand by us now, magister,
Staunch our deep wounds,
Light our dark island,
Heal our sad land.

II

THIS NEUTRAL REALM

Je dis ma mère. Et c'est à vous que je pense, O Maison!
Maison des beaux étés obscurs de mon enfance.

> O. V. de Milocz (1877-1939).

There was a little stream, or brook, never dry, flowing, now slow, now with torrential rapidity, for ever in its narrow ditch. Unsteadily a rustic bridge bestrode its dark waters, a rustic humpbacked bridge, in a state of extreme dilapidation.

> Beckett: *Watt*

I cast a pebble down, to
Set the well's walls echoing.
As the meniscus resettles
I see a strange face form,
A wrinkled female face,
Sweeney's Hag of the Mill,
The guardian of the well,
Source of lost knowledge.

BOG ROYAL

Again, the unwinding road.

Across the Bog of Allen
(a sea of black peat,
our land's wet matrix)
showers mizzling until
over scant brush, necklaced
with raindrops, our reward:
a great cloak torn into
tatters of light, the warm
colours of heather deepened,
dyed to near violet, all
the air trembling, lambent,
— slashes of rain, then sun
with small waves running in
on some reed-fringed island;
Loughs Gowna or Sheelin,
Derravarragh or Finnea.

Come back, Paddy Reilly
to your changed world;
pyramids of turf stored
under glistening polythene:
chalk white power stations,
cleaned swathes of bog,
a carpet sucked clean!
Here the yellow machines
churned roots of bog-oak
like lopped antlers,
the sunken remnants
of the Great Forests
of Ireland, hoarse hunt-
ing horn of the Fianna,

the encumbered elk
crashing through branches,
a houndpack in full cry.

A nomadic world of
hunters and hunted;
beaten moons of gold,
a flash of lost silver,
figures coiling around
a bronze trumpet mouth:
a marginal civilization
shading to the sound
of bells in monastic
sites, above the still
broadening Shannon,
or sheltered on some lake
shore or wooded island:
from Derg to Devenish,
Loughs Gowna to Erne.

A SLIGHT FRAGRANCE

A slight fragrance revives:
cycling through the evening
to a dance in Gowna — Lake
of the Calf, source of Erne —
with one of the Caffrey's.
Our carbide lamps wobbled
along the summer hedges, a
warm scent of hay & clover
as, after the dance, I kissed
my girl against a crumbling
churchyard wall.

                  Our call
at a shebeen on the way back,
black pints by candlelight,
her leg warm against mine,
Barney grinning, with lewd
friendly jokes. I cycled
with her to buy strawberries
from the local big house,
fairy-tale Tullynally;
the Camelot of bogland,
its gothic turrets, stately
descending gardens, always
silvered with river mist.
A bay horse came trotting
down one of the paths, briskly
scattering the first leaves.
Bright spokes almost touch
as we push homewards,
silent dalliance of youth.

The Longford of my childhood,
a harebell lost in heather,
a rumble of donkey carts
across the Inny bridge
to the dwindling mounds
of hand slung turf, a
pony and trap rattling
past to market or Mass,
the view from the Motte
of Granáird over a tranquil
unrushed emptiness, a world
so torpid it woke only to
the tug of the long
church bell rope, the rasp
of a donkey's bray.

RED ISLAND

Time could stop here.

Hidden in the reeds,
a waterlogged boat,
stored by the Reilly's.
We baled it first,
a hull full of green
dead water, clotted
with algae. Then slowly
we poled it, through
crackling walls of reed
with a single oar, to
where the current freed
itself, and the boat
accepts, rides, floats
on the oars' pull into
the brimming full heart
of the sunstruck lake.

A rod triangled against
a summer sky, life narrowed
to the plop of feeding
fish, the sudden flurry
of a bite, huge underjaw
of pike, or light, slim perch,
occasionally the thrash
of some larger fish:
the sun sinking as in
an old legend, *Sionnain*,
the grand-daughter of Ler,
drowned by angry salmon.

Where rats scamper, reeds
gleam like quicksilver,
we land, to gut and broil
our catch. Once, in a haul,
we found a ravenous pike;
inside its stomach, compact as
an embryo, an undigested perch.

We stretch in the grass
to water's lulling murmur.
A ghostly swan dips by;
Fionnuala, lost in her tragedy?
An immense stillness hangs
over Red Island, over
this deep, drowned land
of lobelia, marsh marigold,
a watery graveyard through
which the Inny wanders
its slow weed-choked way
to swell the Shannon.

LAKE DWELLING:CRANNÓG

The sky presses down
metal heavy, a helmet
banding the forehead,
subduing all brightness
to a brackish mist.
No branches stir, with
bird chirp, animal stealth.

We might be the first
to land on this shelf,
hauling up our long
hollowed boats, breaking
a clearing, with the
thick stroke of an axe
on wet wood, plumping

Fat stones, logs down
into the lake's stomach,
smoothing lichen to
floor rough huts of hide
or hacked wattle which
tangle in the wind
stretching & toughening.

The same skins supple
on our naked backs,
our brain a plait
of wet leaves, moss,
our eyes, pinpoints
through drizzle, as
we crouched by a sunken

Cranny, breath tense
for the wary crackle
of a hoof on grass,
an elk's span
of swaying branch;
the round soft eyes
of the musk ox.

SWORD LAND

Still, a violence lurks.
(Recall Blind Tadhg's name
for our land: Sword Land).

Abruptly, a dragon's head
projects from the reeds,
the curling angry prow
of a Viking longship,
serrated wooden fangs
snapping the air, near
Clonmacnoise, Bangor.
Bone biting axes, smoky
resinous torches, plunder
and burn, the flaring
pleasures of destruction!

Or iron knees protruding
below a metal heavy skirt,
the handle of a sword;
holding down Normandy,
hammering down Harold,
a harsh mastery harnessed
by an iron technology.

Their land hungry prows
divide chill waters
for long years before
these sea stained warriors
reconquer our land.

Rehearse Tadhg Dall's phrase
Ferann cloidhimh, crioc Bhanba:
Mountjoy's name for this land —
Ire land: Sword Land?

THIS NEUTRAL REALM

—The great achievement of the South of Ireland
was to stand aside—   *Louis MacNeice*

Here, too, they defied Adolf.
A platoon of the L.D.F.
drilled in the parochial hall,
shouldering Lee Enfields.
A war intimate as a game,
miles better than Indians,
like the splendid manoeuvres
when the regular army came.

We defended Abbeylara
watching the Northern road
— signposts all gone —
from a girdered haybarn,
rifles at the ready,
with dummy cartridges,
until Southern Command
came behind our backs:
took over the town.

So I and my cousin
were captured, condemned
to spend a warm afternoon
incubating in an armoured car,
peering through slits,
fingering the intricacy
of a mounted Brengun.

So we learnt to defend
this neutral realm,
each holiday summer,
against all comers,
including the Allies
if they dared to cross over
(Hitler being frightened).
Eire's most somnolent time
while, at home, invasion
forces risked chilling seas
to assemble in Ulster.

Already seen through
the stereoscopic lens
of a solitary childhood,
our divided allegiances;
a mock and a real war:
Spitfire and Messerschmitt
twinned in fire, Shermans
lumbering through our hedges,
ungainly as dinosaurs while
the South marched its toy
soldiers along the sideline.

THE MUSIC BOX

And now, the road towards Cavan.
Each year, we left you down
by the roadside, Mary Mulvey,
to seek out old relations.
We waited, as you hobbled
away, up that summer boreen.

Mary lived in the leaning
cottage, beside the old well
she strove to keep clean,
bending to skin dead leaves
and insects; ageing guardian
whom we found so frightening

Huddled on the leather seats
of Uncle John's Tin Lizzie
away from your sour, black
shawls, clacking rosary, not
your bag of peppermints, which
we devoured, thoughtlessly.

Maria Marunkey, our hurtful
childish name for your strange
shape, suffering age, its shame
that hooped your back, cramped
and horrible as some toothy witch.
We clattered stones on your roof

Or hunkered whispering past
your half-door, malefic dwarfs,
to startle your curtained silence
with shouts, coarse as farts:
Maria Marunkey married a donkey.
The latch stirs; we scatter, bravely.

Blessedly, you could barely hear,
or begged us in, with further sweets
or gifts, to share your secret.
Nudging, we thronged around
as you laboriously wound —
more creakingly each year —

The magic music box, resurrected
from camphored lace, which ground
out such light, regular sounds,
thawing ice, tinkling raindrops,
a small figure on its rosewood top
twirling slowly, tireless dancer

By its grace, I still remember
you, Mary Mulvey, hobbling along
a summer lane, bent over the well
or shuffling into your cottage,
its gable sideways, like yourself.
Your visits to the home place

To see old friends and neighbours
stopped one year when you were
too crippled to move, and besides;
"There's no one left up there.
They've all died off." A silver
dancer stops. Silent. Motionless.

THE WELL DREAMS

I

*The well dreams;
liquid bubbles.*

*Or it stirs
as a water spider skitters across;
a skinny legged dancer.*

*Sometimes, a gross interruption;
a stone plumps in.
That takes a while to absorb,
to digest, much groaning
and commotion in the well's stomach
before it can proffer again
an almost sleek surface.*

*Even a pebble disturbs
that tremor laden meniscus,
that implicit shivering.
They sink towards the floor,
the basement of quiet,
settle into a small mosaic.*

*And the single eye
of the well dreams on,
a silent cyclops.*

II

People are different.
They live outside, insist
in their world of agitation.
A man comes by himself,
singing or in silence,
and hauls up his bucket slowly —
an act of meditation —
or jerks it up angrily,
like lifting a skin,
sweeping a circle
right through his own reflection.

III

And the well recomposes itself.

Crowds arrive annually, on pilgrimage.
Votive offerings adorn the bushes;
a child's rattle, hanging silent
(except when the wind shifts it)
a rag fluttering like a pennant.

Or a tarnished coin is thrown in,
sinking soundlessly to the bottom.
Water's slow alchemy washes it clean:
a queen of the realm, made virgin again.

IV

Birds chatter above it.
They are the well's principal distraction,
swaying at the end of branches,
singing and swaying, darting excitement
of courting and nesting,
fending for the next brood,
who still seem the same robin,
thrush, blackbird or wren.

The trees stay silent.
The storms speak through them.
Then the leaves come sailing down,
sharp green or yellow,
betraying the seasons,
till a flashing shield of ice
forms over the well's single eye:
the year's final gift,
a static transparence.

V

But a well has its secret.
Under drifting leaves,
dormant stones around
the whitewashed wall,
the unpredictable ballet
of waterbugs, insects,

There the wellhead pulses,
little more than a tremor,
a flickering quiver,
spasms of silence;
small intensities of mirth,
the hidden laughter of earth.

III

THE BLACK PIG

... one sees that the Battle is mythological, and that the Pig it is named from must be a type of cold and winter doing battle with the summer, or of death battling with life.

> W. B. Yeats.

I have arranged to increase the animosity between Orangemen and the United Irish. Upon that animosity depends the safety of the centre counties of the North ...

> General Knox,
> *March 1797.*

THE BLACK PIG

Ballinagh, its flat, main street;
that sudden, sharp turn North.
Nearby, a ridge of the Dunchaladh,
the Black Pig's Dyke, or Race,
— the ancient frontier of Uladh.

Straying through a Breton forest
once, I heard a fierce scrabbling,
saw his blunt snout when,
with lowered tusks, a wild boar
ignored me, bustling past.

And can still believe in
some mythic bristled beast
flared nostrils, red in anger,
who first threw up, where North
crosses South, our bloody border.

(Or some burrowing Worm
slithering through the earth
from Ballinagh to Garrison,
a serpent's hiss between
old Uladh and Ireland.)

And now he races forever,
a lonely fearsome creature,
furrowing a trough we may
never fill, the ancient guardian
of these earthworks of anger.

BORDER LAKE

The farther North you travel, the colder it gets.
Take that border county of which no one speaks.
Look at the straggly length of its capital town:
the bleakness after a fair, cattle beaten home.
The only beauty nearby is a small glacial lake
sheltering between drumlin moons of mountains.
In winter it is completely frozen over, reeds
bayonet sharp, under a low, comfortless sky.
Near the middle there is a sluggish channel
where a stray current tugs to free itself.
The solitary pair of swans who haunt the lake
have found it out, and come zigzagging,
holding their breasts aloof from the jagged
edges of large pale mirrors of ice.

BORDER

That trembling needle
pointing always North.
Approaching our Border
why does my gorge rise?
I crossed it how often
as a boy, on the way
to my summer holidays,
and beyond Aughnacloy
felt a sense of freedom
following the rough roads
through Cavan, Monaghan
greeted at a lakeside orchard
where we stopped to buy
apples, Bramley seedlings,
Beauty of Bath, with
its minute bloodstains.

But by the sand-bagged
barracks of Rosslea, Derrylin
the route is different.
Wearing years later
I go North again and again
— Express bus from Dublin,
long car ride from Munster —
to visit my mother when
she wastes away slowly in
a hospital in Enniskillen:
learn the bitter lesson
of that lost finger of land
from Swanlinbar to Blacklion.

Under Cuilcagh Mountain
inching the car across
a half-bombed bridge,
trespassing, zigzagging
over potholed roads, post-
boxes, now green, now red,
alternately halted by British
patrols, unarmed Garda,
signs in Irish and English,
both bullet-pierced, into
that shadowy territory
where motives fail, where
love fights against death,
good falters before evil.

THE PLAIN OF BLOOD

Near here, he stood,
the Stooped one,
Lord of Darkness,
drinker of blood,
eater of the young,
King of the void,
The Golden Stone.

But are such visions
of an abstract evil
an evasive fiction:
the malignant Cromm
but the warming sun,
his attendant stones
the whirling seasons?

The evil sprang from
our own harsh hearts:
thronged inhabitants
of this turning world,
cramped into a corner,
labelled by legend,
Ulster or Northern Ireland.

Source of such malevolence,
a long-nurtured bitterness.
No Nordic family feud,
arm & thighbone scattered
(*the ravens have gorged
on a surfeit of human flesh*)
but wise imperial policy

Hurling the small peoples
against each other, Orange
Order against Defender,
neighbour against neighbour,
blind rituals of violence,
our homely Ulster swollen
to a Plain of Blood.

THE WEB OF MAN (A CURSE)

A rainfall of blood
from the clouded web
of the broad loom
of man slaughter!
Slate armour grey
the web of our fate
is long being woven:
the furies cross it
with threads of crimson.

The warp, the weft
are of human entrails.
Their severed heads
dangle as weights,
blood dark swords
are spiralling rods.
The arrows clatter
as the furies weave
the web of battle.

The land of Ireland
will suffer a grief
that will never heal.
Men, as yet unknown,
who now dwell upon
wind-lashed headlands
will hold the nation.
The web is now woven:
The battlefield crimson.

—from the old Norse, 11th century.

RED BRANCH (A BLESSING)

Sing a song for the broken
towns of old Tyrone:
Omagh, Dungannon, Strabane,
jagged walls and windows,
slowly falling down.

Sing a song for the homes
or owners that were here today
and tomorrow are gone;
Irish Street in Dungannon,
my friend, Jim Devlin.

Sing a song for the people,
so grimly holding on,
Protestant and Catholic, fingered
at teabreak, shot inside their home:
the iron circle of retaliation.

Sing a song for the creaking branch
they find themselves upon,
hollow from top to bottom,
the stricken limb of Ulster,
slowly blown down.

Sing an end to sectarianism,
Fenian and Free Presbyterian,
the punishment slowly grown
more monstrous than the crime,
an enormous seeping bloodstain.

Sing our forlorn hope then —
the great Cross of Verdun,
Belfast's Tower on the Somme —
Signs raised over bloody ground
that two crazed peoples make an end.

WINTRY DAWN

But who does not fear
      the bristling boar of death
the bustling black
      hog of his own death,
stained tush, with
      all that huge weight
of deadly muscle?
      Hooves pounding in
the reiterated nightmare
      of death drawn O Riada:
breathing and bustling
      out of our dark past
to harry and haunt him:
      the shapely young hero
dying, from thirst,
      his white thigh gashed
under the still brooding
      helm of Ben Bulben,
Fionn, his old friend
      and enemy, near him.

Fionn's hand was stayed
      by a poet, from slaying
the snoring MacMorna;
      Fame lasts longer than
any single life,
      never use treachery:
the poet's morality
      overthrown by jealousy
in this dark valley.
      Three times he allows
the water of life
      to spill from his palms.
Then stands alone.

  Do pale horsemen still
ride the wintry dawn?
  Above Yeats's tomb
large letters stain
  Ben Bulben's side:
Britain, go home!

DEITIES

*From our needs
we create them:
the lean Christ
we help to press,
impale upon the
timbered cross*

*expertly. See us
plant the nails,
marvel at his
blood-streaked
but accepting face,*

*and the gentle
smile of Gautama,
absolving evil,
the lusts, frail
terrors of the flesh.*

*Like St. Francis
he gives away
property right
and left until
a calm shines*

*over our broken
lives, tangled
wills, bitter
battlefields of
society and self.*

*But the old gods
surged from earth,
air, fire, water:
radiant Hermes glid-
ing the light shafts;*

*black extensions
of earth's under-
ground empery of
roots and rocks:
O gloomy Dis!*

*Or from a headland
the sea's power —
a trident finning
the furious waves —
all hail, Poseidon!*

*While the luxuriant
wind caressed grain
of high summer
murmurs of warmth:
O sweet Ceres!*

*

*God or goddess,
they distributed
their favours in
the battle's heat
they stoke so well —*

*tripping Cuchulain,
clouding Achilles
in a psychic confusion
of light and dark:
Balor or Polyphemus,*

*until Ulysses or
Lugh props open
the baleful eyelid,
lunges home with
the burning stake.*

*Abandons, wisdoms;
left to himself,
stripped of creed,
man still faces
the old powers:*

*violence fuming
from some crater,
knows his own dark,
scales his light,
steers his craft.*

IV

THE SILVER FLASK

FIRST CUSTOMER:
>   My mother? My mother was the *real* woman
>   in my life. Every night I pray to her.

SECOND:
>   What about your father? Mine was the
>   berries. But he kept falling off —

>   *Overheard in a Cork pub.*

>   I never haid a mammy
>   she soon gave me up.
>   I never haid a daddy
>   he was always on the sup.
>   I never haid a sweetheart
>   that didn't louse me up
>   so now I'm goin' down,
>   ain't never coming up.

>   *Mountain song.*

Everything that is not suffered to the end and finally concluded, recurs, and the same sorrows are undergone.

>   *Herman Hesse*

GRAVITY

A glimmer of light on
the turning ocean floor;
the moon's white disc
waxing and waning, as
a woman waits, a womb
waits, for the leap
of conception, here in
Ireland, or alien Brooklyn.
The gravity of our child
growing in Evelyn's womb,
unacknowledged, unknown,
while my foresaken mother
wastes glumly away in
a new aseptic hospital
high above Enniskillen;
an exhausted woman, and
a child who will resemble
her, spirits exchanging
in familial communion.

What lonely outcry equals
such a flaring mystery?
Consumed by pain, still
her motherly concern,
enquiring how I had come
so far North again —
just beyond Aughnacloy,
the girdered skeleton
of a burntout Express
I had rushed to catch.
And probing delicately
— where is Madeleine?

so that I might have
sought to explain;
but gentleness forbade.
Should one disturb
the dreams of the old;
her whole life dominated
by an antique code?

NORTHERN EXPRESS

Before Aughnacloy, they are ordered to dismount.
For God and Ulster, he shouts, waving a pistol,
a shadow in the twilight, daft as Don Quixote,
except for that gun stuck in the driver's throat
and brother shadow, sullen in his anorak.
A forced comradeship of passengers tremble
by the sleety roadside, attending sudden death.
Assistant shadow sprinkles petrol leisurely
over the back and sides of the Derry express
while chief shadow asks them to remove their boots,
the classic ritual before a mass execution.
Lucky this time, they are spared, warned off
to tramp behind the driver two miles in the snow
not daring, like Lot's wife, to look for the glow
of their former bus, warming the hedges:
their only casualty, thin socks worn through.

INTIMACY

Mother, mother, I whisper,
over the years we had won
to a sweet intimacy together.
She would come with me often
to Fintona's first picturehouse,
rigged out like a girl friend
in her evening finery, snug
in the best seats, munching
soft centred chocolates. Naturally
we chose Romances, Sir Laurence
stalking the cliffs in *Rebecca*,
Leslie Howard defending the South,
courteous through cannonsmoke,
and I thought I might bring her
to some sad story of Brooklyn,
the bridge's white mirage shining
over broken lives like her own,
but she wept, and dabbed her eyes;
I hate films about real life.

Melancholy destiny, indeed.
Young love, then long separation.
After our drive across Ireland,
my father stood in the kitchen,
surrounded by his grown sons
and the wife he had not seen
for almost two decades, spirit
glass in hand, singing *Slievenamon*
or *Molly Bawn, why leave me pining*,
his eyes straying in strangeness
to where she sat, with folded
hands, gray hair, aged face,

*Alone, all alone by the wave
washed strand,* still his Molly Bawn,
wrought by time to an old woman,
a mournful gnome.

Six years later, he was gone,
to a fairer world than this,
and we sat in television darkness,
searching from channel to channel
while the badmen came riding in,
guns glinting in the prairie sun,
or the pretty nurse fell in love
with the subtle handed surgeon
as the emergency was wheeled in
—*tho' lonely my life flows on*—
and she laughed, reaching down
for the brandy by her side, or
excitedly darting snuff, dust
settling on her apron . . . .

[63]

MOLLY BAWN

Short hair crimped
with curling tongs,
the belle of Fintona's
Cumann na mBan,
haranguing the throng
upon Liskey Brae,
singing rebel songs
on the beach at Bundoran,
knocking the helmet
off a big policeman
with your parasol;
a true Fenian!

His Irish Molly
father called you,
your courtship & wedding
to the sound of marching.
Remember your honeymoon
in troubled Dublin:
a brattle of gunfire
as our pious father
hurries to early Mass
in Newman's Church —
to thank God perhaps? —
the morning after.

Then the long trek
to solace your brothers:
Frank, a medical student
in the Kevin Barry regiment,
interned in Ballykinlar,
Tom, down in the Curragh.

Sprung, after the Treaty,
they serve as officers in
the new Free State Army,
their first national duty
to hunt down old comrades,
split by the Treaty.

Absurdity leads to atrocity;
deserters, after Ballyseedy.
Emigrating anywhere, suburban
England, prohibition Brooklyn,
the embittered diaspora of
dispossessed Northern Republicans
scorning their State Pensions;
a real lost generation. Then
my mother follows her husband,
my future father, off to the New
World, making sure to land in
good time for the Depression!

A MUDDY CUP

My mother
my mother's memories
of America;
a muddy cup
she refused to drink.

His landlady didn't know
my father was married
so who was the woman
landed on the doorstep
with grown sons

my elder brothers
lonely & lost
Father staggers back
from the speak-easy
for his stage-entrance;

the whole scene as
played by Boucicault
or Eugene O Neill:
the shattering of
that early dream

but that didn't
lessen the anguish,
soften the pain, so
she laid into him
with the frying pan

till he caught her
by the two wrists,
*Molly, my love, if
you go on like this
you'll do yourself harm.*

And warmly under
a crumbling brownstone
roof in Brooklyn
to the clatter of
garbage cans

like a loving man
my father leant
on the joystick
& they were reconciled
made another child

a third son who
beats out this song
to celebrate the odours
that bubbled up
so rank & strong

from that muddy cup
my mother refused
to drink but kept
wrinkling her nose
in souvenir of

(*cops and robbers,
cigarstore Indians
& coal black niggers,
bathtub gin and
Jewish neighbours*)

Decades after
she had returned
to the hilly town
where she had been born,
a mother cat,

intent on safety,
dragging her first
batch of kittens back
to the familiar womb-warm
basket of home

(all but the runt,
the littlest one, whom
she gave to be fostered
in Garvaghey, seven miles away;
her husband's old home).

A CHRISTMAS CARD

Christmas in Brooklyn,
the old El flashes by.
A man plods along pulling
his three sons on a sleigh;
soon his whole family
will vanish away.

My long lost father
trudging home through
this strange, cold city,
its whirling snows,
unemployed and angry
living off charity.

Finding a home only
in brother John's speakeasy.
Beneath the stoup
a flare of revelry.
And yet you found time
to croon to your last son.

Dear father, a gracenote.
That Christmas, you did
find a job, guarding a
hole in the navy yard.
Elated, you celebrated
so well, you fell in.

Not a model father.
*I was only happy
when I was drunk*
you said, years later,
building a fire in
a room I was working in.

Still, you soldiered on
all those years alone in
a Brooklyn boarding house
without your family
until the job was done;
and then limped home.

AT LAST

A small sad man with a hat
he came through the customs at Cobh
carrying a roped suitcase and
something in me began to contract

but also to expand. We stood,
his grown sons, seeking for words
which under the clouding mist
turn to clumsy, laughing gestures.

At the mouth of the harbour lay
the squat shape of the liner
hooting farewell, with the waves
striking against Spike Island's grey.

We drove across Ireland that day,
lush river valleys of Cork, russet
of the Central Plain, landscapes
exotic to us Northerners, halting

only in a snug beyond Athlone
to hear a broadcast I had done.
How strange in that cramped room
the disembodied voice, the silence

after, as we looked at each other!
Slowly our eyes managed recognition.
'Not bad' he said, and raised his glass:
father and son at ease, at last.

THE SILVER FLASK

Sweet, though short, our
hours as a family together.
Driving across dark mountains
to Midnight Mass in Fivemiletown,
lights coming up in the valleys
as in the days of Carleton.

Tussocks of heather brown
in the headlights; our mother
stowed in the back, a tartan
rug wrapped round her knees,
patiently listening as father sang,
and the silver flask went round.

Chorus after chorus of the *Adoremus*
to shorten the road before us,
till *we see amidst the winter's snows*
the festive lights of the small town
and from the choirloft an organ booms
angels we have heard on high, with

my father joining warmly in,
his broken tenor soaring, faltering,
a legend in dim bars of Brooklyn
(that sacramental moment of stillness
among exiled, disgruntled men)
now raised vehemently once again

in the valleys he had sprung from,
startling the stiff congregation
with fierce blasts of song, while
our mother sat silent beside him,
sad but proud, an unaccustomed
blush mantling her wan countenance.

Then driving slowly home,
tongues crossed with the communion
wafer, snowflakes melting in
the car's hungry headlights,
till we reach the warm kitchen
and the spirits round again.

The family circle briefly restored
nearly twenty lonely years after
that last Christmas in Brooklyn,
under the same tinsel of decorations
so carefully hoarded by our mother
in the cabin trunk of a Cunard liner.

LAST JOURNEY

                I.M. James Montague

We stand together
on the windy platform;
how sharp the rails
running out of sight
through the wet fields!

Carney, the station master,
is peering over
his frosted window:
the hand of the signal
points down.

Crowned with churns
a cart creaks up the
incline of Main Street
to the sliding doors
of the Co-Op.

A smell of coal,
the train is coming . . .
You climb slowly in,
propped by my hand to
a seat, back to the engine,

and we leave, waving
a plume of black smoke
over the rushy meadows,
small hills and hidden villages —
Beragh, Carrickmore,

Pomeroy, Fintona —
placenames that sigh
like a pressed melodeon
across this forgotten
Northern landscape.

WHAT A VIEW

*What a view he has
of our town, riding
inland, the seagull!*

*Rows of shining roofs
and cars, the dome of
a church, or a bald-*

*headed farmer, and
a thousand gutters
flowing under the*

*black assembly
of chimneys! If
he misses anything*

*it might be history
(the ivy-strangled
O Neill Tower only*

*a warm shelter to
come to roost if
crows don't land*

*first, squabbling;
and a planter's
late Georgian house*

*with its artificial
lake, and avenue of
poplars, less than*

*the green cloth of
our golf-course where
fat worms hide from*

*the sensible shoes
of lady golfers).
Or religion. He may*

*not recognise who
is driving to Mass
with his army of*

*freckled children —
my elder brother —
or hear Eustace*

*hammer and plane
a new coffin for
an old citizen,*

*swearing there is
no one God as the
chips fly downward!*

*He would be lost,
my seagull, to see
why the names on*

*one side of the street
(MacAteer, Carney)
are Irish and ours*

*and the names across
(Carnew, MacCrea)
are British and theirs*

*but he would understand
the charred, sad stump
of the factory chimney*

*which will never burn
his tail feathers as
he perches on it*

*and if a procession,
Orange or Hibernian,
came stepping through*

*he would hear the
same thin, scrannel
note, under the drums.*

*And when my mother
pokes her nose out
once, up and down*

*the narrow street,
and retires inside,
like the lady in*

*the weather clock,
he might well see
her point. There are*

*few pickings here,
for a seagull, so
far inland. A last*

*salute on the flag
pole of the British
Legion hut, and he*

*flaps away, the
small town sinking
into its caul*

*of wet, too well
hedged, hillocky
Tyrone grassland.*

V

A FLOWERING ABSENCE

> . . . I am re-begot
> Of absence, darkness, death; things which are not.
>
> John Donne

> Mother, you had me but I never had you
> I wanted you but you didn't want me
> So I got to tell you
> Goodbye goodbye
>
> John Lennon

FAMILY CONFERENCE

When the wall between her and ghost
Wears thin, then snuff, spittoon,
Soothing drink cannot restrain:
She ransacks the empty house.
The latch creaks with the voice
Of a husband, the crab of death
Set in his bowels, even the soft moon
Caught in the bathroom window
Is a grieving woman, her mother
Searching for home in the Asylum.
What awaits, she no longer fears
As dawn paints in the few trees
Of her landscape, a rusty shed
And garden. Today grandchildren
Call, but what has she to say
To the buoyant living, who may
Raise family secrets with the dead?

PROCESSION

i.m. Grandmother Hannah Carney

Hawk nose, snuff stained apron;
I stand beside you again in
the gloom of your hallway
peering up & down Fintona's
cattle stained Main Street
some thronged fairday evening.

As you ramble on, like someone
sick or drunk, confessing to
a stranger in a bar, or train;
ignoring my small years while
you spell out your restless pain,
mourn a tormented lifetime.

Frank, your pride, eldest boy,
interrogated again and again,
arrested in your warm kitchen,
bayonets and British voices
bullying him abruptly away
to the barbed wire, the tin

huts of Ballykinlar, model
for Long Kesh, Magilligan.
Your youngest son, Tom, then
drills in the old bandroom
to follow him; soon lands
himself into the Curragh prison.

Released, your two internees
were met at the railway station,
cheered and chaired home
with a torchlight procession:
but one half of the town
held its blinds grimly down.

Still hatred and division
stain that narrow acre
from which you sprang.
A half century later
the same black dreams
return to plague your daughter,
their sister, my mother.

A Paisleyite meeting
blared outside her window.
A military helicopter
hovered over the hospital,
a maleficent spider. Her
dying nightmares were of her
sons seized by soldiers!

Across the rough, small hills
of your country girlhood —
the untamed territory of
the Barr, Brougher Mountain —
we brought your daughter home,
yellow car beams streaming;
a torchlight procession.

NORTHERN LIGHTS

*Northwards stream the wild
geese, through the long Polar
night (the bewildered cries
of the newly dead, shocked
spirits hurled out of life)
with the slow flap of wide
thunderous wings lured by
an ultimate coldness, that
magnetic needle wavering,
trembling always North.*

On the funeral morning
I wrench from dark dream
to find my cousin's arm
looped loosely over mine.
We dress and drive down
the seven long miles that
separated me from mother
and brother, Montague
from Carney, fading farm
from stagnant small town.

In my hostile imagination
chill rain always beats down
on these small gray houses,
only gay on market days,
the ballad-singer's voice
raised in rough song:
*On top of Old Smokey,
all covered with snow,
I lost my own true love,
by courting too slow.*

A stranded community,
haunted by old terrors,

the Dromore murders;
neither Irish, nor British,
its natural hinterland
severed by the border:
doleful men lounging
along the station wall;
Golfcourse and Carnival,
the effort to seem normal.

Here my mother lived
where her mother lived
before her, endlessly
toiling narrow stairs,
endlessly raking over
the cold ashes of
her neighbour's foibles,
marginally living, and
obsessed with dying,
now finally achieved.

The ceremony, soon over;
no ritual graces the event,
a lifeless modern funeral
without music or song,
to lament the dead, or
ease the living. No piper
struts, or kneels down,
with swelling resonance,
no slow fiddle lifts, to
sweeten our burden.

A few clods clump down
and now she lies again
with our father, near
her own mother, while
across the fresh grave
an upright relative tries

hard to slight me, but
I want no truck with
this narrowing world
of bigotry and anger.

Each death is our own:
a child of seven, as
dawn drew in, I would
lie awake, singing &
sighing to myself, *I
am I, and I must die;*
recognizing the self as
I feared the end of it:
the spirit fretting in-
side the body's casket.

Consciousness, a firefly
sparkling with cognition,
living through a thousand
minor deaths, as the atoms
of the body decay, separate,
to be endlessly rewoven,
endlessly reborn, my body
of seven years ago, shed;
this final death, a freedom;
a light battling through cloud.

*By whistling you could
bring them nearer —
or so I was often told.
A magnetic storm of
particles, a sperm
shower of the sun,
violent sounds haunting
lost Polar expeditions —
our sky's virid necklace,
the Northern Lights.*

A FLOWERING ABSENCE

How can one make an absence flower,
lure a desert to sudden bloom?
Taut with terror, I rehearse a time
when I was taken from a sick room:
as before from your flayed womb.

And given away to be fostered
wherever charity could afford.
I came back, lichened with sores,
from the care of still poorer
immigrants, new washed from the hold.

I bless their unrecorded names,
whose need was greater than mine,
wet nurses from tenement darkness
giving suck for a time,
because their milk was plentiful

Or their own children gone.
They were the first to succour
that still terrible thirst of mine,
a thirst for love and knowledge,
to learn something of that time

Of confusion, poverty, absence.
Year by year, I track it down
intent for a hint of evidence,
seeking to manage the pain —
how a mother gave away her son.

I took the subway to the hospital
in darkest Brooklyn, to call
on the old nun who nursed you
through the travail of my birth
to come on another cold trail.

Sister Virgilius, how strange!
She died, just before you came.
She was delirious, rambling of all
her old patients; she could well
have remembered your mother's name.

Around the bulk of St. Catherine's
another wild, raunchier Brooklyn:
as tough a territory as I've known,
strutting young Puerto Rican hoods,
flash of blade, of bicycle chain.

Mother, my birth was the death
of your love life, the last man
to flutter near your tender womb:
a neonlit barsign winks off & on,
motherfucka, thass your name.

There is an absence, real as presence.
In the mornings I hear my daughter
chuckle, with runs of sudden joy.
Hurt, she rushes to her mother,
as I never could, a whining boy.

All roads wind backwards to it.
An unwanted child, a primal hurt.
I caught fever on the big boat
that brought us away from America
— away from my lost parents.

Surely my father loved me,
teaching me to croon, *Ragtime Cowboy*
Joe, swaying in his saddle
as he sings, as he did, drunkenly
dropping in from the speakeasy.

So I found myself shipped back
to his home, in an older country,
transported to a previous century,
where his sisters restored me,
natural love flowering around me.

And the hurt ran briefly underground
to break out in a schoolroom
where I was taunted by a mistress
who hunted me publicly down
to near speechlessness.

So this is our brightest infant?
Where did he get that outlandish accent?
What do you expect, with no parents,
sent back from some American slum:
none of you are to speak like him!

Stammer, impediment, stutter:
she had found my lode of shame,
and soon I could no longer utter
those magical words I had begun
to love, to dolphin delight in.

And not for two stumbling decades
would I manage to speak straight again.
Grounded for the second time
my tongue became a rusted hinge
until the sweet oils of poetry

eased it and light flooded in.

THE LOCKET

Sing a last song
for the lady who has gone,
fertile source of guilt and pain.
The worst birth in the annals of Brooklyn,
that was my cue to come on,
my first claim to fame.

Naturally, she longed for a girl,
and all my infant curls of brown
couldn't excuse my double blunder
coming out, both the wrong sex,
and the wrong way around.
Not readily forgiven,

So you never nursed me
and when all my father's songs
couldn't sweeten the lack of money,
when poverty comes through the door
love flies up the chimney,
your favourite saying,

Then you gave me away,
might never have known me,
if I had not cycled down
to court you like a young man,
teasingly untying your apron,
drinking by the fire, yarning

Of your wild, young days
which didn't last long, for you,
lovely Molly, the belle of your small town,
landed up mournful and chill
as the constant rain that lashes it,
wound into your cocoon of pain.

Standing in that same hallway,
don't come again, you say, roughly,
I start to get fond of you, John,
and then you are up and gone;
the harsh logic of a forlorn woman
resigned to being alone.

And still, mysterious blessing,
I never knew, until you were gone,
that, always around your neck,
you wore an oval locket
with an old picture in it,
of a child in Brooklyn.

A NEW LITANY

I

The impulse in love
to name the place as
protection and solace;
an exact tenderness.
The way a room
can be so invested
with the presence
of a capable woman:
I see you bustling
around the house,
fragile and living,
tensely loving, as
long ago, my mother.
May she be granted,
this houre, her Vigill,
a certain peace.

II

That we are here
for a time, that
we make our lives
carelessly, carefully,
as we are finally
also made by them;
a chosen companion,
a home, children;
on such conditions
I place my hopes
beside yours, Evelyn,
frail rope-ladders
across fuming oblivion.

III

A new love, a new
litany of place names;
the hill city of Cork
lambent under rain,
the lamenting foghorn
at Roche's Point, hold-
ing its hoarse vigil
into a white Atlantic,
the shrouded shapes
of Mounts Brandon,
Sybil Head and Gabriel;
powers made manifest,
amulets against loneliness,
talismans for work:
a flowering presence?

BACK

At the other end
of Ireland, a boat
is waiting, trestled
high above sand
and stone. A woman
is waiting, asleep
in a sunlit room —
our first haven —
above the Atlantic's
heaving lung.

In an adjoining room,
curled in her cot
our first child draws
her honeyed breath;
a slighter rhythm.
One more death, and
the generation older
than Brendan and myself
will have gone to earth.

'To walk away, without
looking back, or crying':
an old Inuit saying,
simple folk wisdom.
The rites duly performed,
goodbyes decently said,
honour satisfied, we
head back across the
length of Ireland, home.